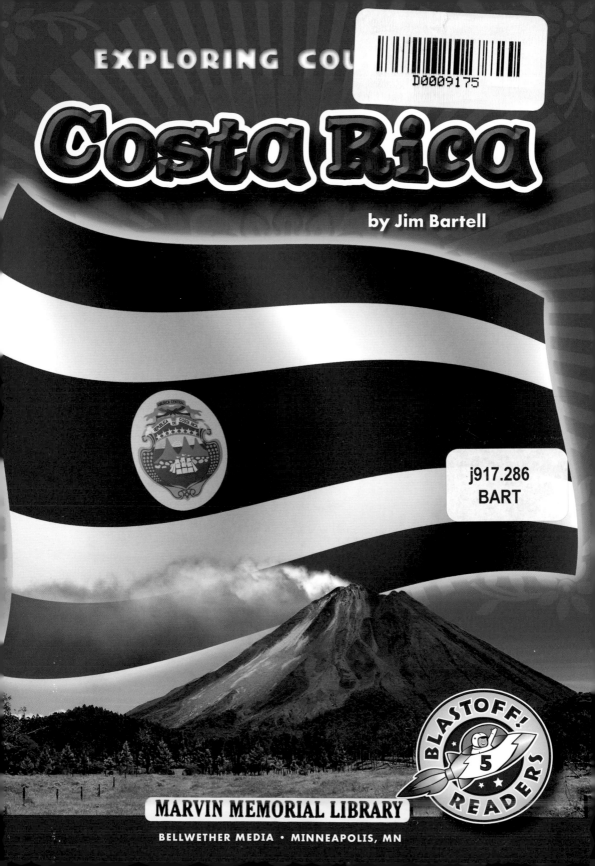

EXPLORING COU

Costa Rica

by Jim Bartell

BLASTOFF! 5 READERS

BELLWETHER MEDIA · MINNEAPOLIS, MN

Note to Librarians, Teachers, and Parents:

Blastoff! Readers are carefully developed by literacy experts and combine standards-based content with developmentally appropriate text.

Level 1 provides the most support through repetition of high-frequency words, light text, predictable sentence patterns, and strong visual support.

Level 2 offers early readers a bit more challenge through varied simple sentences, increased text load, and less repetition of high-frequency words.

Level 3 advances early-fluent readers toward fluency through increased text and concept load, less reliance on visuals, longer sentences, and more literary language.

Level 4 builds reading stamina by providing more text per page, increased use of punctuation, greater variation in sentence patterns, and increasingly challenging vocabulary.

Level 5 encourages children to move from "learning to read" to "reading to learn" by providing even more text, varied writing styles, and less familiar topics.

Whichever book is right for your reader, Blastoff! Readers are the perfect books to build confidence and encourage a love of reading that will last a lifetime!

This edition first published in 2011 by Bellwether Media, Inc.

No part of this publication may be reproduced in whole or in part without written permission of the publisher. For information regarding permission, write to Bellwether Media, Inc., Attention: Permissions Department, 5357 Penn Avenue South, Minneapolis, MN 55419.

Library of Congress Cataloging-in-Publication Data
Bartell, Jim.
Costa Rica / by Jim Bartell.
     p. cm. – (Exploring countries) (Blastoff! readers)
Includes bibliographical references and index.
Summary: "Developed by literacy experts for students in grades three through seven, this book introduces young readers to the geography and culture of Costa Rica"–Provided by publisher.
ISBN 978-1-60014-572-8 (hardcover : alk. paper)
1. Costa Rica–Juvenile literature. I. Title.
F1543.2.B37 2011
972.86–dc22   2010039124

Printed in the United States of America, North Mankato, MN.

010111   1176

Contents

Nicaragua

Costa Rica

San José ★

Pacific Ocean

Did you know?
Costa Rica is Spanish for "rich coast."
Explorers from Spain gave it this name
because they believed they would
find a lot of gold in the country.

Caribbean Sea

Panama

Costa Rica is a small country in Central America. It covers 19,730 square miles (51,100 square kilometers) and borders two other countries. Nicaragua lies to the north, and Panama sits to the southeast. At Costa Rica's narrowest point, the Pacific Ocean and the Caribbean Sea are only about 75 miles (120 kilometers) apart. The country also includes several small islands, some of them hundreds of miles from the coast. The capital is San José, which is located in central Costa Rica.

Costa Rica is a land of mountains, rivers, forests, and beautiful coasts. **Rain forests** fill the country's southwestern region and stretch along the Caribbean coast. **Cloud forests** cover many mountains throughout Costa Rica. In the northwest, tropical dry forests are full of trees that lose their leaves in the driest time of year.

Mountain ranges run the length of the country. Many have active volcanoes. Rivers begin in the mountains and flow into the **lowlands** near the coasts. Off the coasts lie large coral reefs, which are home to many plants and animals.

Did you know?
The Arenal Volcano in northwestern Costa Rica was dormant for 400 years before it erupted in 1968. Since then, it has erupted several times and lava continues to flow from it.

Did you know?

The Monteverde Cloud Forest Reserve receives almost 118 inches (3 meters) of rain every year.

Costa Rica has many national parks and wildlife reserves. The most famous reserve is the Monteverde Cloud Forest Reserve, located in northwestern Costa Rica. Established in 1972, the reserve now covers almost 41 square miles (105 square kilometers).

A soft mist blankets the forest. It is caused by the cool, moist winds from the Caribbean Sea. The winds sweep up the mountainsides, and the cold air causes the moisture to **condense** into a fog. Through the mist, visitors can see the many kinds of wildlife that call the reserve home.

fun fact

The Monteverde Cloud Forest Reserve has a hummingbird gallery. Visitors can see more than 30 kinds of hummingbirds.

mantled howlers

Costa Rica has many different **habitats** that support a wide range of wildlife. Four kinds of monkeys swing from tree to tree in different forests. Mantled howlers live in groups of up to 40 monkeys and howl to talk to each other.

giant anteater

jaguar

fun fact
The giant anteater lives in Costa Rica. It has a long, thin tongue that it uses to capture ants and termites. A giant anteater can eat thousands of ants and termites every day.

Sloths hang from trees in the rain forest. Below, pig-like animals called tapirs roam the forest floor. They both must watch for dangerous jaguars, Costa Rica's largest **carnivores**.

More than 4.5 million people live in Costa Rica. Nine out of every ten Costa Ricans have **ancestors** from Spain. Some also have ancestors who were **native** to the land of Costa Rica. People with mixed backgrounds are called *mestizos*. Along the Caribbean coast, a small group of people has ancestors who were **immigrants** from Jamaica.

A few native tribes live in Costa Rica's highlands. The Bribri are the largest tribe. All of the tribes have their own traditions and speak their own languages. Most Costa Ricans speak Spanish, the country's official language.

Speak Spanish!

English	Spanish	How to say it
hello	hola	OH-lah
good-bye	adiós	ah-dee-OHS
yes	sí	SEE
no	no	NOH
please	por favor	POHR fah-VOR
thank you	gracias	GRAH-see-uhs
friend (male)	amigo	ah-MEE-goh
friend (female)	amiga	ah-MEE-gah

Many Costa Ricans live in the countryside. They live in **adobe** houses on farms or in towns. Although many towns now have supermarkets, most people buy their food fresh every day from vendors at street markets or small shops. Those who own cars can travel to cities if they need items they cannot find in their towns.

In cities, most people live in apartment buildings. Some live in houses in the **suburbs**. People often shop at street markets in their neighborhoods. They use buses and cars to get from place to place.

Where People Live in Costa Rica

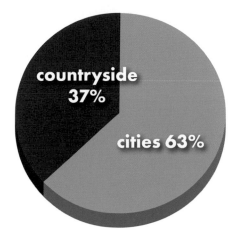

countryside 37%

cities 63%

In Costa Rica, children must attend school until they are 16. However, some families in the countryside are unable to send their children to school. They cannot afford the books, uniforms, and other supplies. Those who do attend school start in elementary school. They move on to secondary school when they are 12 years old. After that, they must pass tests in different subjects in order to attend a university. Costa Rica has five public universities for students to attend. Students can also go to private universities.

Where People Work in Costa Rica

services 64%

manufacturing 22%

farming 14%

Most Costa Ricans have **service jobs**. They work in schools, banks, and other places that serve people. They run hotels, museums, and national parks for **tourists**. Factory workers make chemicals, food products, and other goods. Ships bring these goods to countries around the world.

In the countryside, farmers grow coffee, pineapples, and bananas. These are the three main crops in Costa Rica. Farmers also grow melons, corn, and beans. Some raise cattle and **poultry**. Along the coasts, fishermen catch fish that are sold to markets. Others raise fish in tanks on **fish farms**.

Did you know?
Lake Arenal, the largest lake in Costa Rica, is a favorite place for windsurfers to go for a ride!

The beautiful Costa Rican landscape gives people many reasons to go outside. People enjoy kayaking and rafting on the country's lakes and rivers. Hikers, mountain climbers, and mountain bikers explore the trails throughout the country. Surfers hit the beach to catch big waves along the Pacific coast.

Soccer and baseball are popular sports. Many towns have their own teams that compete in nationwide leagues. Art and dance are also important parts of Costa Rican culture. People especially like to dance to *soca*, *salsa*, and *bachata* beats. Large cities such as San José have theaters and cinemas where people go to see plays and movies.

Did you know?
Refrescos are Costa Rica's most popular cold beverages. To make one, fresh fruit is mixed with a small amount of sugar and either milk or water.

Costa Rican food is mild compared to the food of other Central American countries. Instead of using hot spices, cooks use garlic and **herbs** to season dishes. The national dish is *gallo pinto*, or rice with black beans, cilantro, onions, and sweet peppers. It is usually enjoyed at breakfast with eggs, tortillas, coffee, and juice. For lunch and dinner, Costa Ricans often enjoy a *casado*. This meal includes rice, black beans, fried **plantains**, a small salad, a tortilla, and meat.

fun fact

Along the Caribbean coast, people cook seafood with coconut milk and vegetables to make *rondon*, a famous Caribbean dish.

rondon

gallo pinto

Independence Day

In Costa Rica, many holidays celebrate the country's history. Independence Day falls on September 15. Costa Ricans crowd the streets to dance, sing, and celebrate their independence. Another important holiday falls on July 25. On this day in 1824, the people of an area called Guanacaste chose to become part of Costa Rica.

Most Costa Ricans are Christians and celebrate Easter and Christmas. Another important Christian holiday in the country is Lady of the Angels Day on August 2. On this day, thousands of **pilgrims** travel to the city of Cartago. There, they worship Costa Rica's **patron saint** at the Basilica of Our Lady of Angels.

Basilica of Our Lady of Angels

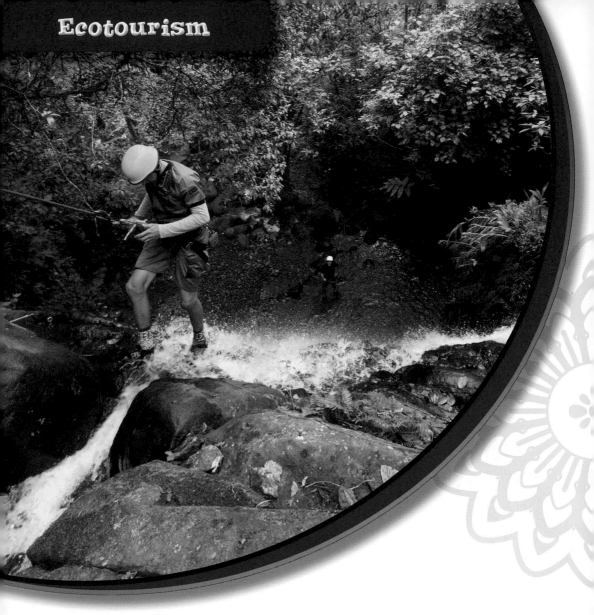

Costa Ricans work hard to protect their country's natural environment. They want to share it with people from around the world. Ecotourism is a responsible way for tourists to enjoy the Costa Rican landscape. The country has created many parks and reserves that welcome visitors. Hunting, logging, and mining are not allowed in these areas.

Many Costa Ricans work in these parks and reserves. They show tourists the country's plants and animals while keeping the environment safe from harm. Costa Ricans take pride in their effort to preserve the land for others to enjoy. Through ecotourism, Costa Rica teaches the importance of preserving natural wonders.

Did you know?
The motto of ecotourism is: "Take nothing but pictures, leave nothing but footprints, and waste nothing but time."

Fast Facts About Costa Rica

Costa Rica's Flag

The flag of Costa Rica has five horizontal stripes. The blue stripes at the top and bottom represent the sky and opportunity. The two white stripes stand for peace, happiness, and wisdom. The middle of the flag has a thick red stripe that stands for the blood shed for freedom. This stripe also holds the country's coat of arms. The current design was adopted in 1906.

Official Name: Republic of Costa Rica

Area: 19,730 square miles
(51,100 square kilometers);
Costa Rica is the 129th
largest country in the world.

Capital City:	San José
Important Cities:	Alajuela, Cartago, Heredia, Limón
Population:	4,516,220 (July 2010)
Official Language:	Spanish
National Holiday:	Independence Day (September 15)
Religions:	Christian (92%), Other (8%)
Major Industries:	farming, fishing, manufacturing, services, tourism
Natural Resources:	fish, farmland, wood
Manufactured Products:	computer parts, food products, clothing, chemicals, plastics, medical equipment, construction materials
Farm Products:	coffee, bananas, pineapples, melons, sugarcane, rice, beans, corn, beef, poultry, dairy products
Unit of Money:	colón; the colón is divided into 100 céntimos.

Glossary

adobe—bricks made of clay and straw that are dried in the sun

ancestors—relatives who lived long ago

carnivores—animals that eat only meat

cloud forests—forests at high elevations that are often covered in fog

condense—to change from a gas into a liquid, usually because of cooling

fish farms—farms that raise fish in large tanks; fish farms sell fish to markets and restaurants.

habitats—environments in which particular plants or animals usually live

herbs—plants used in cooking; most herbs are used to add flavor to food.

immigrants—people who leave one country to live in another country

lowlands—areas of land that are lower than the surrounding land

native—originally from a specific place

patron saint—a saint who is believed to look after a country or group of people

pilgrims—people who travel to a holy place to worship

plantains—tropical fruits that look like bananas; plantains are often eaten fried in Costa Rica.

poultry—birds raised for their eggs or meat

rain forests—thick, dense forests that receive a lot of rain

service jobs—jobs that perform tasks for people or businesses

suburbs—communities that lie just outside a city

tourists—people who are visiting a country

To Learn More

AT THE LIBRARY

Collard III, Sneed. *Forest in the Clouds*. Watertown, Mass.: Charlesbridge, 2000.

Deady, Kathleen W. *Costa Rica*. New York, N.Y.: Children's Press, 2004.

Shields, Charles J. *Costa Rica*. Broomall, Penn.: Mason Crest Publishers, 2009.

ON THE WEB

Learning more about Costa Rica is as easy as 1, 2, 3.

1. Go to www.factsurfer.com.

2. Enter "Costa Rica" into the search box.

3. Click the "Surf" button and you will see a list of related Web sites.

With factsurfer.com, finding more information is just a click away.

Index